CHILDREN
of the
MINES

**A BOOKLET PRODUCED
FOR THE
CYNON VALLEY HISTORY SOCIETY
BY
D. L. DAVIES B.A.**

**TO COMMEMORATE
150 YEARS
OF
COAL
IN THE
CYNON VALLEY,
1837 – 1987**

©
1987
Cynon Valley History Society
ISBN 0 9508586 4 1
Printed by REPRINT, CARDIFF

'. . . ac wele ddagrau y rhai gorthrym-
edig . . . ac ar law eu treiswyr yr oedd
gallu, a hwythau heb neb i'w cysuro'.

— Ecclesiastus 4, ad. 1.

The Cynon Valley History Society has for its objects to promote, encourage, and maintain an active interest in the history of the district in all its aspects: to arrange appropriate talks and lectures; to organise visits to places of interest in the locality and elsewhere; to undertake original research and assist in the collection of local material such as manuscripts, books, photographs, etc.; and to publish books on local history.
The Society meets on the third Thursday in each month and membership is obtained simply by contacting the Hon. Secretary, Mr J F Mear, 7 Tudor Terrace, Aberdare CF44 8EB.

FOREWORD

by the Mayor of the Cynon Valley,
Cllr. Mrs. P. Jarman

I am happy to have been asked to write a short Foreword to this new publication by the Cynon Valley History Society.

The Society has already done a great deal to preserve and publicize the history of our valley, and they are to be congratulated on their work. However, I find it hard to imagine anything they could have produced that would have been more timely than this present booklet.

It is intended to commemorate the sinking of the first deep mine in the area at Cwmbach in 1837. In this, the Society brings to mind all the dramatic developments which followed this venture, and which transformed our valley from being an isolated rural district into a major centre of industrial activity in the space of a few decades.

In tracing the growth and decline of the coal industry there is a danger for historians sometimes to neglect the human side of the story.

I am delighted this has not been so in this case. In choosing to publish details of the employment of children and young people in this area in 1841, the Society has picked out a most human story. Some of the things revealed here that youngsters were then put through are almost beyond belief; yet they did happen — sometimes to children as young as 7 and 8 years of age.

I recommend this new publication to you. If you read it you may be shocked; you may be angered. You *will* be moved.

Yours sincerely,

PAULINE JARMAN
Mayor of the Cynon Valley, 1987-88

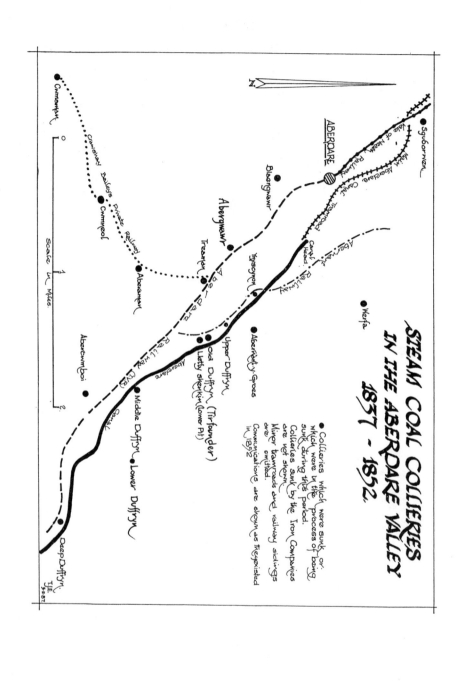

STEAM COAL COLLIERIES
IN THE ABERDARE VALLEY
1837 - 1852.

● Collieries which were sunk, or
which were in the process of being
sunk, during this period.
Collieries sunk by the Iron Companies
are not shown.
River tramroads and railway sidings
are omitted.
Communications are shown as they existed
in 1852.

T.J.E
3207

THE EARLY BACKGROUND TO COAL MINING IN THE CYNON VALLEY

This year marks the 150th anniversary of sinking the first deep coal mine in the Cynon Valley the purpose of which was not to service the fuel needs of local ironworks but to produce a commodity saleable in its own right. It is this intent which lies behind the term 'sale-coal' just as use of the term 'sea-coal' recognized that its journey to the wider market was often undertaken by coastal cargo vessels.

The long and eventful story of the sale-coal industry in the Cynon Valley may therefore be said to have begun that day in June, 1837 when the Wayne family of Gadlys ironmasters had their workmen start sinking the shaft of their Abernant-y-groes colliery at Cwmbach. It was the beginning of a momentous chapter in the history of this valley as all such initial ventures were in those other valleys of south Wales where the deep mining of coal got underway in the early- and mid-19th century.

The exploitation of the region's coal measures was a huge undertaking in terms of the labour, capital and engineering involved. It transformed the idea of Wales both within and beyond its own limits. It had a profound impact upon the economy and politics of Britain and even of the world. It has been said that a far-flung British empire was physically held together by the power of Welsh steam coal in the boilers of its navy; and that Britain probably sailed in triumph out of one world war by virtue of the same resource. Nor does this overlook the contribution of the south Wales coal trade towards turning the wheels of domestic industry, where its clean burn and steam producing qualities were especially appreciated. The Aberdare district lay at the heart of this steam coal trade, and its continued growth until the First World War took the name and produce of this valley as of others across the world.

For this reason, and in commemoration of all those who toiled in the industry to make it such a success (though not necessarily for themselves), the committee of the Cynon Valley History Society thought it appropriate to mark the 150th anniversary in a suitable fashion. This booklet is a practical means to that end. It does not pretend to be a history of the coal trade in the valley. Such a *magnum opus* must await other times and probably several authors. Yet this present booklet is a small contribution towards telling the story of our people in this place during an era when 'King Coal' reigned supreme. In that sense, it complements those other essays relating to the history of the coal industry in the district which the Society has already published between 1976 and 1985 in the first four volumes of its main publication, *Old Aberdare*.

The coal society which 19th century developments created was one marked by every emotion and fortune imaginable, often on a broad region-wide scale. Yet this ought not to lead towards forgetting the thousands of individuals who bore these great changes in humble obscurity: sometimes knowing good fortune; sometimes surviving by the sheer heroism of individual or collective will. Tragedy, exploitation, endless toil, deprivation, despair, anger; but also hope, idealism, loyalty, faith, humour and the pursuit of learning all passed each other on the busy streets of a town like Aberdare and its surrounding villages during the coal years.

Now, the industrial environment of that society has either gone or is vanishing rapidly. It is good to see the worst aspects of those years fall away; but it is the hope of many that the finest human qualities of that society which coal created should survive among us, and that lessons drawn from its experience should not be lost to us by disregarding the evidence which survives.

The best values of the 'coal society' can only be appreciated if we know something of the pressures and forces that created it. In this, nothing is likely to surpass the impact of testimony gathered in 1841 in south Wales (as elsewhere) concerning the employment of children and young people in mines and places of manufacture. That is why it was decided to include in this commemorative booklet salient points from the main report covering south Wales which repeatedly draws upon information gained at Hirwaun; and also to include full details of the evidence given here by individuals who met the two sub-commissioners sent to Aberdare. Apart from three professional figures at Hirwaun (a surgeon, school-master and nonconformist minister), the words printed recall the voices of the working people themselves. The *Report* of the Commission of Inquiry, published in 1842, is the first social document out of which ordinary people of the time speak for themselves. This makes the source additionally worthwhile.

Local evidence to the Children's Employment Commission was chosen for this booklet because of its special poignancy, but also because it dates from a time only four years after the sinking of the first deep colliery at Abernant-y-groes. Purists might point out that the Commission's report centres at Aberdare upon people working in and for ironworks and not sale-coal mines like those the Waynes and Thomas Powell of the Gaer had newly sunk in the district. This is true; but the reason for it is simply that sale-coal mining was such a new departure whereas ironworking by 1841-42 had almost a century of tradition behind it (the Hirwaun works having been started in 1757). It is a sufficient answer to such purists to point out also that much of the mining done on behalf of the ironworks was of coal: a point obvious in the Aberdare evidence.

This present booklet would not wish to commemorate the sale-coal trade exclusively when mining iron ore and coal for smelting were such closely related industrial experiences. The booklet is therefore a means of commemorating 1837 and *all* it evokes. For it should be borne in mind that coal mining of one kind or another has a history at Aberdare dating back far beyond 1837 or even the rise of Hirwaun in 1757. This is borne out by manorial and other legal documents which mention digging for coal in the vicinity of Aberdare from the late 16th century onwards.

A booklet such as this does not provide enough opportunity to note in detail all the extremely interesting references that survive concerning early coal mining in the area, and a few allusions must satisfy until some future occasion.

The renowned Glamorgan antiquary Rice Merrick, writing in circa 1578, made general mention that in both the upland *(blaenau)* and lowland *(bro)* regions of the county there were 'mines of iron, lead, tin and coal'. Probably the first specific mention of coal mining in the Aberdare district is that lease of the 29th August 1578, by which Thomas Howell of Llantrisant and his sons were granted by the earl of Pembroke as lord of the manor of Miskin the right to work coal on an area of land called Y Wern, being part of the lord's demesne (or reserved) property known as Tir Llwyn y Bedw. By 1583 it is said that a 'coal pit' was working there. In 1596, Thomas Howell was still at work in the locality, and rented an unnamed plot for 5 shillings per annum which was probably still at Tir Llwyn y Bedw. This demesne land was situated at Llwydcoed, and formed part of the ancient manorial extent of 'fforest Llwydcoed'. Other parts of Tir Llwyn y Bedw, as well as further manorial land known as Gwaun y Person (situated towards the crest of the mountain above Llwydcoed) were leased from the earl by one Thomas Griffith; and he, in turn, sub-let some of his rights to an individual named William John Lewis. The latter was said in 1588 to be cutting coal at Tir Llwyn y Bedw by virtue of this sub-lease.

The families of Thomas Howell and Thomas Griffith seem to have been among the most persistent of the early coal exploiters in the area. By manorial surveys of 1630 and 1638 which list the interests of the Pembroke family in Glamorgan one learns that Thomas Griffith was still leased of coal deposits at Tir Llwyn y Bedw and Gwaun y Person; and he had added another plot known as Pen Rhiw Mynydd to these. It was said of him in 1638 that 'Thomas Griffith houldeth the Coale Mynes in Aberdare', and that 'there are Coale Mynes upon the Lord's demeane land called Gwayne y p'son and Tire y lloyn Bedw within ye parishe of Aberdare'. Also in 1638, Jevan Thomas Howell is recorded as holding part of Gwaun y Person for life at an annual rent of 3s. 4d, and part of Tir y Llwyn Bedw for 6s. 10d.

On the 20th September, 1631 the earl of Pembroke granted to Thomas Mathew of Castell Mynach, near Llantrisant (a kinsman of the Mathew family of Aberaman), leases of land mostly towards Llantrisant 'together with ye libertye of digging cole veines upon ye premises'. Among the outlying tracts thereby leased was 'all that parcell of waste ground in ye severall lordships of Miskin and Glynrouthney called Tir Wayne Wrgan, to be taken . . . as the sd. Thomas Mathew shall thinke fitt'. This 'Tir Wayne Wrgan' recalls the full form of the ancient name by which the upper reaches of the Cynon Valley had been known since documentary evidence begins in the year 1203; i.e. Hirwaun Wrgan.

This conveyance refers to coalmines already established upon the 'waste ground', and allowed Mathew the right 'to make any new pitt for his owne use and benefitte'. It was added as a part of the agreement that 'the within-mentioned parcell of waste lande called Tir Wayne Wrgan and the cotts thereupon erected, as aloe the libertye of digging coale and stone on the same, are not valued by reason that the sd. Thomas hath not nor could not make any benefitt thereof'. Without further comment it is revealing to note the reference to 'cotts thereupon *erected*', and to the liberty of digging coal which it is inferred Mathew had already employed without much financial reward.

There are numerous other references to mining coal in the Aberdare district which date from the 17th century and 18th centuries, but they must be put aside for the while since the observation regarding Mathew's limited success in 1631 raises another important point. This concerns the local and largely domestic scale of primitive operations. The two parish histories that appeared in the volume *Gardd Aberdar* (1853) illustrate the restricted nature of pre-industrial coal digging very well. The following passage comes from the first of these essays and makes the point in relation to the 1790s:

> A seam of coal approximately 22 inches thick was worked at the top end of Craig y Dyffryn . . . and when the small amount of earth which covered the coal seam would collapse, the collier would open a new level; . . . a man by the name of R.P. Jenkin got hold of the same vein at Cwmpenor, but this coal did not suit the purpose of roasting oats, so that the Dyffryn miller was compelled to get scorching coal from the top of Gellideg moorland in the parish of Merthyr Tydfil, and it was half a day's work to carry one two hundredweight load of it on horseback. The few inhabitants who resided here at that time received the little coal which was essential to them from Llanfabon and from the Darrenddu. There was a small coalworks on the Ynyslwyd land also.

(*Old Aberdare*, vol. 2, page 47)

One other very human source which reflects the working of coal in this district prior to the 19th century is the series of local parish registers. These commence in 1734; and at irregular intervals they mention occasional colliers, miners or people connected with them. There are some eleven such references in the Aberdare registers during the 18th century. The first records the baptism on the 15th March, 1741 of Jane, 'daughter of Jenkin the Coalier'; the last notes the burial on the 11th October, 1799 of Morgan, 'the son of late Thomas Morgan, miner'. There are some nine further references between 1800 and 1809; and from 1810 there are usually two or three such per year. This fact signifies the gradually increasing presence of mining as an occupation among the inhabitants of the parish.

In drawing these introductory remarks to an end I should like to thank a number of people for their help in producing this most recent publication of the Cynon Valley History Society.

Firstly, thanks are due to the *Illustrated London News* for co-operating with the Society in publishing here contemporary pictures of Thomas Powell's Middle Dyffryn colliery, Cwmbach, used by the I.L.N. in May, 1852 at the time of an explosion in those works whereby 65 people lost their lives. The willingness of the present Mayor of the Cynon Valley, Cllr Mrs Pauline Jarman, to contribute a foreword to this booklet is also much appreciated.

In addition, particular thanks are due to members of the committee of the Society: to its secretary, John Mear, who first proposed the idea of a commemorative title; to Tom Evans for providing a map of major local collieries and the list of accidents in the appendix; to Steven Graham for every assistance in his role as Reference Librarian at Aberdare Central Library; and also to Doug Williams, the Society's publications officer, for invaluable help in providing illustrations which support the text so appropriately. Finally, my thanks to the committee as a whole for having entrusted to me the task of compiling this work.

D.L. DAVIES,
October, 1987

EXTRACTS FROM THE REPORT OF SUB-COMMISSIONER ROBERT HUGH FRANKS, ESQ., CONCERNING THE EMPLOYMENT OF CHILDREN AND YOUNG PERSONS IN THE COLLIERIES AND IRON-WORKS IN SOUTH WALES, AND THE CONDITION OF SUCH CHILDREN AND YOUNG PERSONS:

(SOURCE: Appendix to the Report of the Royal Commission of Enquiry into the State of Children in Employment, 1842; Vol. III, Part II, pp.469-491):

EDITOR'S NOTE:

The Royal Commissioners of Enquiry appointed two sub-commissioners to assist them by gathering evidence directly on their behalf in and about the mines and manufacturing works of south Wales during the year 1841. A third sub-commissioner was appointed in respect of north Wales. The two officers for south Wales were Robert Hugh Franks and Rhys William Jones. Both submitted reports to the Commissioners and appended detailed evidence from named individuals in support of their submissions. The testimonies gathered by both in the vicinity of Aberdare are reproduced here in full. Of the two reports submitted, that of R.H. Franks is by far the more broadly-based and wide-ranging. It touches a great many points and succeeds in providing a general view of the circumstances in which the labouring population of the region lived at that time. While obviously sympathetic to many of the needs of the people with whom he came into contact, Franks nevertheless displays that hierarchical view of the social order which might be expected of one in his position during this period. He also reveals the tendency of those in authority at the time to regard the Welsh language as at best an archaism and at worst an obstacle to improvement. His remarks upon nonconformity also retain an air of that dubiousness with which the Establishment long regarded religious dissent. It is only fair to add, however, that at no stage do his comments approach the disdain conveyed by the Commissioners of Enquiry into the State of Education in Wales who took up their work five years later in 1846-47. The numbers which appear in brackets after the following extracts refer to the paragraphs in Franks' report from which those statements are drawn.

I   AGES AND NUMBERS:

In the divisions in which the ages of those employed in the collieries . . . are . . . classed there is no provision for the entry of the . . . ages of young children under the age of 13 years; I, however, considered it my duty to make special inquiries into this branch of the subject, and . . . you will find in the evidence . . . sufficient . . . instances to enable you to appreciate the very early age at which it is the practice to take children down to work in the mines; and . . . it can scarcely be said to be . . . uncommon . . . for a child to work at the early age of five years and a half – this is the youngest age at which I myself have found any employed; but Mr Thomas Joseph, mineral agent of the Plymouth Works, Merthyr Tydfil,[1] . . . states 'children are employed as air-door keepers at 5 years of age; as horse-drivers at 14, as colliers at 12 years of age'. (4)

II PLACES OF WORK:

... the mines in South Wales are, for the most part, entered by level ... the hilly character of the country and the mineral lying in many instances so near the surface presenting facilities for this mode of working. In others ... the mines are entered by shafts, and the coal is transported from the pit-bottom either by the common windlass, by steam or by a balance-wheel ... As the balance-wheel is somewhat peculiar to this country, a brief description may ... . be acceptable ... The descending-cage, charged with water, by its weight brings to the surface the coal in the opposite cage, and when it reaches the bottom of the pit is discharged of its water, which drains down the level ... The coal thus brought to the surface is transported to the level road by inclines, which, acting upon a similar principle of balance by an endless chain, bring up the empty trams for those loaded with coal, the power being gained by the weight of the descending train. Some of these inclines are of great length[2] ... (8-9)

As the state of the pits differs in proportion to the ... attention ... bestowed upon the operations ... and the ... advantages or disadvantages of the locality ... so is the labour of the collier, haulier and air-boy more or less irk-some; where a want of attention is ... combined with natural disadvantages the situation of all employed is distressing. In some few pits lads were ... employed as pumpers, which ... is ... cold, fatiguing, painful and productive of rheumatic affections. (10)

In working the mines of iron-ore in patches, that is to say, where the ore is found within a few feet from the surface, and the opening is made from the surface, girls are very frequently employed in wheeling and otherwise assisting the workmen; they are called patch-girls, or girls who work in the patches; they lead a sort of half-savage life. Hardy, and exposed to all kinds of weather, they work as hard as the men, from whom they differ but little in dress and quite equal in grossness.[3] (15)

III NATURE OF EMPLOYMENT:

The particular labour in which children and young persons are employed in the collieries is of three kinds: colliers, horse-drivers or hauliers; air-door boys; and, in some collieries, carters and skip-haulers. The duty of the haulier is to drive the horse and tram, or carriage, from the wall-face where the colliers are picking the coal to the mouth of the level. He has to look after his horse, feed him in the day, and take him home at night: his occupation requires great agility in the narrow and low-roofed roads; sometimes he is required to stop his tram suddenly — in an instant he is between the rail and the side of the level, and in almost total darkness slips a sprig between the spokes of his tram-wheel, and is back in his place with amazing dexterity; though it must be confessed ... he frequently gets crushed. The haulier is generally from 14 to 17 years of age, and his size is a matter of some importance according to the ... height and width of main roads. As a class these youths have an appearance of greater health than the rest of the collier population (probably from their being more in the fresh air than the others), with fair animal spirits; and on horseback, going to or returning from work, galloping and scrambling over the field or road, bear the aspect of the most healthy and thoughtless of the collier-boys. (16-18)

The air-door boy is generally from five to eleven years of age: his post is in the mine at the side of the air-door, and his business is to open it for the haulier, with his horse and tram, to pass, and then to close the door after them. In some pits the situation of these poor things is distressing. With his solitary candle, cramped with cold, wet, and not half-fed, the poor child, deprived of light and air, passes his silent day: his or her wages 6d to 8d per day. Surely one would suppose nothing but hard poverty could induce a parent so to sacrifice the physical and moral existence of his child! Yet I have found such to be the case arising as frequently from the cupidity as from the poverty of parents. (19)

IV HOURS OF WORK:

In the collieries of South Wales the hours of work are generally from six in the morning until six at night, including the time given to meals; and as in collieries and iron-works the labour of children and young persons accompanies the labour of the adult workmen, their hours of labour are of the same duration as the labour of the men. In the iron-works, the process of . . . manufacture . . . being continuous and the blast-furnaces being kept at work night and day, the attendants on those furnaces work night-shifts — the men and women . . . take alternate night- and day-work of 12 hours. (45-46)

V MEALS:

The children and young persons employed in collieries generally take to their work bread and cheese for their meal . . . for which, however, no fixed time is set aside. The haulier eats his food as he drives his horse along; the little air-door boy may take his meal when he pleases; and as the colliers are paid per ton for their work, they too choose their own time. A supper, however, is generally provided for the collier's return, of bacon and vegetables most usually, for the colliers rarely eat much fresh meat during the week. In the iron-works two rests are allowed for two meals in the course of the day . . . (49-50)

VI TREATMENT AND CARE:

The industry and cleanliness of the female population of South Wales, particularly in the county of Glamorgan, are apparent in their persons and homes; and I am led to believe that their children, in infancy, are the objects so tender maternal solicitude; and if the Welsh mother knew the dangers which awaited the physical constitution of her child by its exposure to the foul air of the colliery at the immature age of *five* years, no legislative enactment would be required to limit the age at which the boy should commence work. In general, the Welsh women are remarkable for attention to warm clothing, which they secure for themselves in woollens, flannels, etc; nor are they less anxious for their husbands and children — the men and children are always well defended against the general inclemency of the mountain country. On the return from work it is usual for the workmen and children to be washed; in fact, in lodging houses it is part of the bargain that the lodger shall be washed every night previous to retiring to rest; a point which . . . is strenuously insisted on by the housekeeper. At five years of age, however, arises the call for labour; to add an extra half-crown a week to the wages of the father the child is sent into the mine. From this period the mother seems to consider herself relieved from the responsibility of the treatment and care of her child; that child follows a new teacher, a new instructor. The father or the employer becomes the object of his imitation; he drinks, smokes and swears, the child follows his example, and children of seven years of age and even less will be found to enter in their expenses at the shop their supply of tobacco: and the evidence will show that swearing, drinking and obscene language are vices too frequent amongst the young. Education is a subject to which the working people seem to attach little value. Ignorant themselves . . . they cannot appreciate the value of that education of which they themselves never knew the want. The consequence is that the children, if they go to Sunday-school, are sent rather as a mark of respect to those who recommended education than from any esteem for the benefits to be derived from instruction. Parents are careless of the attendance of their children at school . . . (51)

It is much to be lamented that few or no efforts are made to facilitate a change in the habits of the manufacturing and mining population of South Wales . . . As matters stand . . . in the largest manufacturing town (Merthyr Tydfil), the working man after labour has no resort but the beer-shop; his boy accompanies him, his daughter often passes the evening there. . . . it is surely a source of deep regret that a small portion of the enormous wealth of the land . . . should not be applied to the improvement of the moral and educational condition of its inhabitants — the productive sources of that wealth. (53)

Of the girls it may be said that, although perhaps the age at which they commence labour, except as air-door girls, is not so early as that of boys, their usefulness in the house to assist the mother . . . is a plausible reason for their being kept away from school. At eight or nine years she will be found either a tip girl or piler in the iron-works, or some corresponding employment . . . and as she advances in years she finds some new labour open to her. . . . freedom from restraint after labour . . . induces young girls to labour in the iron and other works in preference to entering domestic service — the complaint of the difficulty of obtaining domestic servants . . . is very frequent . . . (54).

Intemperance seems rarely to be the vice of the women of South Wales; and however frequent and early the connexion of the sexes may be, the cases of bastardy are comparatively trifling; it being usual . . . for a youth to marry a girl when discovered to be pregnant by him. Many instances of improvidence occur, as may be expected from such early marriage — a mere child of 14 years of age becomes a wife, and her first important act is to open an account at the shop for goods, clothing, food, etc. This facility of procuring goods to the credit of her husband's labour induces extravagance . . . and . . . increased expenditure. (55-56)

VII HIRING AND WAGES:

The usual mode of hiring in collieries (and) iron-works . . . in South Wales is by the month. In many instances . . . the younger hands are employed by the man and not by the master, and the terms on which they are hired are of course determined by the adult whom they assist, and in the collieries the collier boy is, to all intents and purposes, the property of his father (as to wages) until he attains the age of 17 years or marries; his father receives his wages whether he be an air-door boy of five years of age or a haulier of 15. (57-58)

A very absurd custom exists among the colliers in South Wales . . . of . . . being allowed privileges of work for a male child taken into the mine; in some instances indeed the same privilege is claimed for girls. At the collieries at Hirwaun and some others, as I am informed, no matter the infant's age, strength or capacity, into the mine he must be taken to enable his father to claim an extra tram of coals: that is to say, supposing . . . the quantity of coal desired to be raised being limited the full day labour of a collier (was) not . . . required . . . the system of privileges seems to have been devised, and by this means the married man works for . . . a full day . . . giving the man with a family a chance of extra work . . . (59)

In many parts of Glamorganshire . . . the wages of the working collier population are very rarely paid in money, but a shop in the neighbourhood, not professedly in the hands of the proprietors of the works, advances goods to the workmen employed in the mine on account of the proprietors; the books of the shop and the books of the colliery are checked on the pay-day at the same office, and the balance, if any, is handed over to the men. It very often happens, however, that the men unfortunately have nothing to receive for months together. It is said by many that the necessaries of life are dearer in these shops by 25% than in others perhaps five miles off; but whether this is the case or not I cannot decide; but I am convinced that the system adopted has a very pernicious effect on the independent means of subsistence of the labouring population, since there is rarely any balance in the hands of the workmen to apply in the purposes of education . . . The system as at present carried on is much felt by the working people themselves, and is the subject of frequent complaint by them; . . . and I cannot but consider it highly disadvantageous to the children as well as the men.[4] (60 & 62)

The average rate of wages in the iron-works during the last five years may be stated as follows:[5]

Year:	Colliers:	Miners:[6]
1837	£1.2s.6d.	£0.19s.7d.
1838	£1.4s.0d.	£1. 1s.3d.
1839	£1.7s.0d.	£1. 1s.3d.
1840	£1.4s.0d.	£0.19s.3d.
1841	£1.2s.0d.	£0.17s.3d.[7]

J.C. Woolrige, Cashier to the Plymouth Works.

The average rate of collier's day wages in the months of March, April and May in the years specified:

1837	3s.10¾d.
1838	3s. 2½d.
1839	3s. 8 d.
1840	3s. 8¾d.
1841	3s. 7½d.

VIII PHYSICAL CONDITION:

. . . I beg to refer to the evidence of the medical gentlemen . . . from which it will be seen: That amongst colliers the diseases most prevalent are chronic diseases of the respiratory organs, especially asthma and bronchitis, arising probably from inhalation of atmosphere charged with carbon, etc; That those who labour in the iron-ore mines are affected with chronic diseases of the chest . . . and . . . are *more frequently* the subjects of consumption than colliers. (63-65)

I have not been able to ascertain for want of sufficient data the average duration of a collier's life in . . . Glamorgan . . . but it is admitted that such *average duration* is *less* than that of a common labourer.[8] . . . On the subject of employment of children in mines at a very early age . . . Charles Forest (sic), surgeon to the Hirwaun Iron-Works, writes: 'Most undoubtedly the employment of very young persons under ground will have a tendency *per se* to *engender disease* by deteriorating the powers of the system, and so *shorten the duration of life*'. (67 & 75-76)

This testimony of medical gentlemen, and of managers and overseers in various works . . . proves that the . . . health and strength of children and young persons is deteriorated by their employment at . . . early ages . . . in the works . . . enumerated; and . . . that their opportunities of intellectual, moral and religious culture are diminished. (85)

IX ACCIDENTS:

I was desirous of ascertaining the whole number of accidents that have happened in the different mines and works which I have personally visited; But it is much to be regretted that an apparent unwillingness to communicate exists amongst those who alone are capable of affording the requisite information. At present, it should seem, no record whatever is kept of accidents, either by the medical gentleman who is invariably attached to each work or in any of the books of the particular firm. (86)

. . . in cases of fatal accidents which . . . have not been of sufficient magnitude to rouse public attention, many difficulties lie in the way of obtaining an impartial inquiry, from the jury in many instances being selected from the fellow-workmen of the deceased, and who are unwilling to hear, even if they think it necessary to call, evidence which may possibly involve either their employer or anyone employed in the same work with themselves . . . in mining districts, the workmen formed the juries, and, as a matter of course, none could be found to return verdicts or levy deodands, by which their employers would be injured . . . The mode of conducting inquests . . . as at present is more injurious than useful: proprietors and culprits escape . . . (90 & 92)

X MORAL CONDITION:

. . . in some districts, the slender means of education placed within reach of the working classes, and in others the neglect to avail themselves of the means placed before them, has produced a state of ignorance greatly to be lamented . . . in most instances education ceases when labour commences: . . . I cannot refrain from observing that great neglect appears to prevail in the different Sunday-schools in the various districts, which, although very numerous, seem to me to be most inefficient if I am to judge of their worth by the scriptural knowledge possessed by those children . . . in the habit of attending . . . them regularly . . .[9] (96 & 107).

Before quitting this branch of the subject, I cannot forbear remarking that I regard the want of culture of the English language as one great obstacle to the improvement of the people . . . However much we may admire . . . patriotism . . . of history and . . . language, . . . when . . . the language of the laws under which the nation is governed, and in which the business of the country is . . . transacted is English, the study of . . . English . . . becomes . . . imperative . . .[10] (109-110)

The numerous chapels . . . built and which are . . . building, . . . and the general attendance of the population . . . on the Sabbath, manifest a strong religious tendency in the people; and their subdued and orderly appearance on the Sunday . . . indicates a . . . respect for . . . religion: the professors [11] are said to exercise great control over the habits as well as the religious tenets of each particular congregation . . . and I am further informed that they exercised a salutary counsel on the occasion of the late outbreaks.[12] (111)

Benefit societies, under the name of friendly societies, are very numerous amongst all classes of the working population, . . . nor are these clubs monopolized by the men, the females in many places forming small societies regulated on similar principles . . . The object of these societies is to provide . . . for the relief of members when sick or out of work, as also for the burial of deceased members. It is said that a very strong prejudice conceived against the New Poor Law Bill has given an impulse to the establishment of these societies, which by their rules and orders have, in the opinion of many, produced great improvement in the habits and morals of the colliers and manufacturers, as well as the female part of the population . . .[13] (112)

The number of licensed houses in the manufacturing district is much complained of, and apparently not without reason; I myself have seen not less than *six* in a row, next door to each other, and although I have not any returns on this subject to lay before you, my own conviction is that they do a great deal of harm . . .[14] (114)

As affecting the health and comfort of a working population, few subjects are more important than the situation, structure and drainage of their houses. The situation of houses inhabited by colliers in the county of Glamorgan is generally on the side of a hill, from the hilly character of the country; and as the drainage is almost universally neglected, they are much affected by the heavy rains to which South Wales is particularly exposed, and which pour in torrents down the mountain sides. (119)

Indeed it would be very difficult to find many collier communities where the drainage can be said to be good: . . . and the absence of privies, etc., amongst the labouring population manifests a want of appreciation of comfort in domestic arrangements. . . . and it is the more remarkable where houses are built by the proprietors themselves for the people employed in their collieries and mines that such arrangements are not made . . . But perhaps the most miserable hovels inhabited by the working people are to be found in the neighbourhood of the Hirwaun Works, and they derive a more comfortless appearance from the barren surface of the plain in which they are situated. Many of these are nothing more than mud-cabins, in many instances a deserted cow-shed converted into a human habitation; a rude thatch forms the roof and, apparently to avoid the storms that sweep along that plain, they are built in every hollow that can be found where of course they receive the drainage of the surrounding elevations. Hirwaun itself . . . is bordered by a range of lofty hills, and is in many parts boggy and full of water. A more cheerless place could scarcely be found in South Wales: even the school which I visited here more resembles a stable than a place for education, and is almost surrounded with a ditch of dirty water. But it is not alone . . . even in the large and populous manufacturing town of Merthyr Tydfil no general system of drainage is adopted; no water is supplied to the population . . .[15] (122)

From . . . the collected evidence and . . . attentive inquiry into . . . subjects distinguished in this Report, I submit . . . the following points . . . (1) That labour in the collieries of . . . South Wales . . . is unwholesome and productive of diseases which . . . shorten life or reduce the . . . years of useful labour . . . (2) That the physical health and strength of children and young persons are deteriorated by their employment at the early ages . . . before enumerated. (3) That the education, both secular and religious, of the children of the working population is lamentably defective, the means of instruction very small, and the slender opportunities afforded . . . diminished by the early age at which children commence working. (4) That a restriction of the age at which children should be allowed to labour in the mines and works should be fixed, and young girls altogether excluded from such labour; and . . . that an educational qualification to labour should be established throughout the mining . . . district of South Wales . . . (123-128)

ROBERT H. FRANKS
London, December 20th, 1841

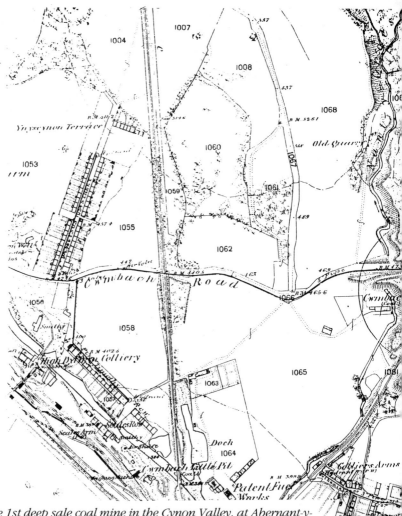

1. The site of the 1st deep sale coal mine in the Cynon Valley, at Abernant-y-
    Groes, Cwmbach. Sinking began in June 1837; and by December, the 4'
    seam was reached and exhibited in London. Partners in the venture
    (undertaken in the name of the Aberdare Coal Company) were the Wayne
    family of the Gadlys Ironworks; William Thomas David of Abernant-y-
    Groes Uchaf; and the executors of Morgan Thomas David of Abernant-y-
    Groes Isaf. Although W.T.D. was apparently the active head of the David
    family, it appears from an examination of the 1844-47 tithe Map of the
    Parish that the pit was sunk in the furthermost corner of a field belonging to
    the Abernant-y-Groes Isaf property, where it abutted another farm known
    as Cwm Bach, belonging to the Marquis of Bute. Prior to the sinking the site
    seems to have been one of woodland pasture simply designated "Coed".
    The tenant of the 'Isaf property at the time was Llewelyn Howells, 1806-
    1857, [the third great grandfather of the present editor].
    Source: 1875 25" O.S. Map, surveyed in 1868.

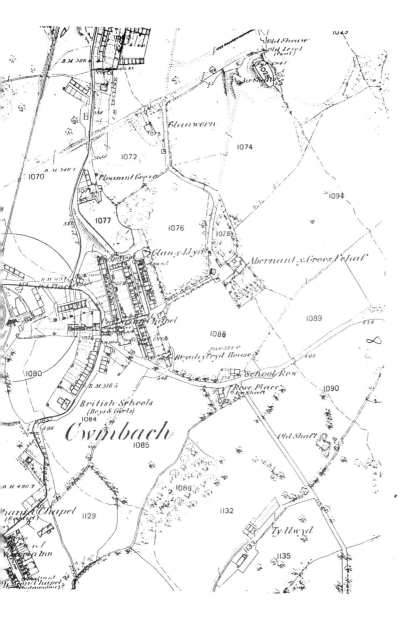

2. *Two rule books belonging to local friendly societies based at Hirwaun. The Welsh handbook relates to the Cambrian Lodge of the Oddfellous Order meeting at the Bodwigiad Arms. The Lodge had been established on the 3rd September, 1828.*
Source: D.L. Davies

FOOTNOTES:

1   In 1841, Thomas Joseph was clearly still mineral agent to the Plymouth Ironworks with which his grandfather, Morgan Joseph, had been closely associated before him; in 1842, however, he began his career as a developer of the coal trade by opening a level at Dan-y-deri, Merthyr, in conjunction with his brother-in-law, Samuel Thomas. In 1849, they transferred their coal interests to the Aberdare valley and opened that year the Ysguborwen colliery (now the site of the Pirelli factory, Trecynon). They also started together the Bwllfa colliery, Cwmdare possibly as early as 1851. In 1858, Joseph became bankrupt and was bailed out by his father-in-law, the local coalowner, David Davis of Blaengwawr. Thereafter, Joseph redirected himself to the Rhondda valleys and sank collieries which eventually formed a part of the Dunraven United Collieries Co. (Morris & Williams, *The South Wales Coal Industry, 1840-1875*, Cardiff, 1958, pp.129-130 and 154-155). Joseph was a mining engineer of note during his day, and he also ventured at one time into chapel architecture. He designed Heol-y-felin Baptist chapel, Trecynon, which was completed in 1852 for the (then) large sum of £920. The interior of the chapel retains its original, lettered iron pillars and is a fascinating period-piece. It was said of Joseph that he designed 'several Baptist chapels' locally, though his other works are not confirmed. Certainly there is no other structure quite like the squat, top-heavy exterior of Heol-y-felin which was described as his masterpiece (*Llawlyfr Undeb Bedyddwyr Cymru*, Aberdar, 1915, pp.49–59).

2   There was one such long and steep incline at Cwmaman. This conveyed loaded and unloaded waggons between the Cwmaman Colliery's mineral line on Mynydd Coedcae (opened in 1850-52) and those sidings of the Aberdare Railway (opened in 1845-46) which extended along the floor of the Aman valley as far as the site of Cwmneol colliery (David Lloyd, *Hanes Cwmaman*, Aberdar, 1913, p.7). The course of this incline has long since been covered over by spoil from Cwmneol colliery; but its existence was recalled in the name of the first street of industrial housing built in the Aman valley — Incline Row. This was ascribed the name 'Cwmaman Houses' by the enumerator of the 1861 census, and was largely demolished in about 1960 (though one building still stands).

3   D.T. Alexander, a resident of Aberdare during the 1850s, described the appearance of girls who worked in the local ironworks by saying: 'they used to dress in fustian trousers with short skirts down to the knee, and these were made of a rough canvass material, with jackets something like a short coat put over their shoulders, and with large leather pads strapped on to their backs for pushing backwards the trams along the tramways. On their heads they wore flat straw bonnets or hats which were very like those worn by cockle women. These they wore not only at the works, but about the streets also' (*Glamorgan Reminiscences*, reprinted Barry, 1973, p.39). David Lloyd, in writing his *Hanes Cwmaman* in 1912, wrote (p.7) of local girls that worked above and below the pit surface in the mid-19th century, and added that 'some of them live in Cwmaman today' (translation).

4   For a discussion of the truck-shop system at Aberdare see R. Ifor Parry, 'Early Industrial Relations in Aberdare', in *Old Aberdare*, vol. 3, Cynon Valley History Society (C.V.H.S.), 1984, pp.15-17.

5   Surrounding notes in the original indicate that these are weekly rates.

6   In the Children's Employment Report of 1842 as elsewhere a general distinction is made between the term 'collier' (signifying one who dug coal for whatever purpose) and 'miner' (signifying one who mined iron-ore).

7   The changing average weekly rate reflects the practice among employers of conceding wage rises or enforcing cuts according to variable trade patterns. There is obviously a difficulty in relating these figures to today's values. It may be useful to recall that in 1971, when the present decimal currency was introduced, 12 old pence equalled 1 shilling; 1 shilling equalled 5 new pence; and 100 new pence

made £1. A further problem exists in that the value of £1 in 1837 would have been very different to the value of £1 in 1987. One useful comparison recently made estimates that the £1 of 1883 would have been worth only 3½ pence in 1983 · (David Egan, *Coal Society,* Welsh Office, 1987, pp.150-151).

8   This may well have been so as a result of the perils of industry; but it was the other side of the coin by which industrial workers were paid (truck permitting) significantly more than they had received in those rural districts which most of them had but recently left. That is why so many made the change by migrating to the south Wales coalfield from neighbouring rural counties and from further afield. As an aspect of the evidence collected for the Children's Employment Commission in Glamorgan and Carmarthenshire during September, 1841, sub-commissioner R.W. Jones quoted the approximate weekly earnings of a number of industrial and agricultural workers. In comparison to the industrial incomes noted above, Jones records that three agricultural labourers he had encountered at Llan-non and Llangennech, Carms., aged 23, 28 and 41, received weekly wages of about 10s., lls. and 12s. respectively (pp. 706-707).

9   There were no doubt great differences of attainment in the voluntary Sunday Schools at work among the labouring poor of south Wales at this time; but Franks' comments here should be balanced by many of those made by assistant-commissioner William Morris in 1847 when he visited on behalf of the Commission of Inquiry into the State of Education in Wales a good number of Sunday Schools in mining districts. Instances of workers being amazingly well-educated in matters of faith following their attendance at nonconformist Sunday Schools were quoted by Morris at Llansamlet, Llantwit Fardre and Pontypridd to name but a few of many possible cases. So much so that the Commissioner for Glamorgan was himself moved to remark that he had 'heard much of the knowledge possessed by the Welsh labouring classes in the abstruser points of Christian doctrine . . .'; and that 'It will be seen from several . . . Reports that . . . teachers or scholars knew a good deal on these points; and that . . . in a systematic form' (*Report* of the Commission, Part I, London, 1847, p.332: footnote. See also the remarks of John Dixon, schoolmaster at the Hirwaun Ironworks school, in 1841 to sub-commissioner R.W. Jones, reproduced below.).

10   It is surely permissible for a Welsh historian to suggest that Franks' remarks at this point represent not objective logic but an imperial presumption. It might be thought more logical to have had the laws, government and business of a country conducted in the language of that country so that they might be understood by its people. That this was never attempted during the 19th century seems both a part of the tragedy of Wales and an aspect of manipulating workers towards well-ordered subservience.

11   'Professors' was one of several disdainful terms of long-standing used by Anglicans to describe dissenting ministers of religion. It enabled them to avoid giving nonconformist clergy use of the term 'minister' as this was a title Anglican clergy still revered in relation to their own calling.

12   It is not certain which 'late outbreaks' Franks has in mind here. The Merthyr Rising of 1831 had occurred just ten years before; and the Chartist march on Newport just two years previously in 1839. More likely, however, are those strikes which broke out among the colliers of south Wales between May and September, 1840 in resistance to an enforced reduction of wages (Morris & Williams, op.cit., pp.248-249).

13   The New Poor Law had been enacted since 1834 and was hence no longer a Bill. Its essential tenet was to discourage the payment of outdoor relief and to provide indoor relief in parish (or union) workhouses of such a basic nature that none but the truly desolate would consider becoming a charge on the local poor rate. On the subject of friendly societies at this time, see Gwyn A. Williams, 'Friendly Societies in Glamorgan, 1793-1832', in the *Bulletin* of the Board of Celtic Studies, vol. XVIII, part III, (November, 1959), pp.275-283.

14   For an account of licensing and licensed premises at Aberdare, see Richard Arnold, 'The Pubs, Clubs and Breweries of Aberdare', in *Old Aberdare*, vol. 2, C.V.H.S., 1982, pp.107-126.

15   Precisely the same situation existed at Aberdare as in Merthyr until the middle of the 1850s. T.W. Rammell's *Report* of 1853 to the General Board of Health in London described graphically the insanitary conditions which prevailed throughout the parish of Aberdare and which encouraged the spread of typhus, small-pox and cholera morbus among the population. Rammell's *Report* is reproduced in full in *Old Aberdare*, vol. 1, C.V.H.S., 1976, pp.33-55. To improve matters, a Local Board of Health was established in 1854; and this, in effect, was the forerunner of the later urban district council and of today's borough council.

3. *The Rev. William Williams, 1807-1877, minister of Nebo Independent Chapel, Hirwaun, and a witness before the Employment Commission of 1842 (Franks' evidence no. 308) and the Education Commission of 1847.* Source: *"Hanes Eglwys Annibynol Ebenezer," Aberdâr, 1898, pp.18/19.*

EVIDENCE COLLECTED BY SUB-COMMISSIONER ROBERT HUGH FRANKS, ESQ., IN RESPECT OF HIRWAUN* COLLIERY AND IRON-WORKS, COUNTY OF BRECON, MESSRS. CRAWSHAY, PROPRIETORS:

(SOURCE: Appendix to the Report of the Royal Commission of Enquiry into the State of Children in Employment, 1842; Vol. III, Part II, pp.551-554):

NUMBER OF PERSONS EMPLOYED:

Adults . . . .

Young persons under 18 years of age . . . .

Under 13 years of age . . . .

(Upon application to Mr William Jones, cashier of these works, for the necessary information required under the Commission, he stated that, not having received any orders to that effect from the proprietors of the works, he regretted he was not in a position to offer me any assistance. I found it necessary therefore to pursue my inquiries in a different direction, and the result will be seen from the following evidence.)

Population of the village of Hirwaun about 2,000: the majority dependent for employment on the coal and iron-works.

NO. 308 REV. WILLIAM WILLIAMS, minister of the Independent Church, Hirwaun:[1]

I have been four years minister of this place. My congregation consists of a large number of Welsh and some few English, chiefly employed in the iron and coal-works. I occasionally address the English in their own language, but most usually preach in Welsh. There are at present many girls working in the mines, which is pernicious to their morals, and totally disqualifies them for domestic duties: it corrupts their minds, and makes them callous to religious impressions; in fact, until the establishment of Sunday-schools the people were very dark (ignorant) in these parts. The majority of the females here are unacquainted with the English language, and, from the continual contact with men of coarse habits, become as degraded as the most vulgar of the male population.

Children go very young into the mines, which certainly does injure their health, and they always have a less healthy appearance than those who work above ground. I cannot speak of the actual state of health of the people, but I know there is a good deal of consumption here, and many are afflicted with rheumatism. Many of the cottages are built on very low ground, and no attention whatever is paid to the drainage.

There are five Sunday-schools in operation here: two with the Independents, one with the Baptists, one with the Wesleyans, and one with the Calvinistic Methodists. The average attendance at my school is about 200, teachers and scholars.

There is one day-school for boys, but I do not think there is any female school: the attendance at the day-school is about 50.

Children generally leave at eight years of age to go to continuous employment. I think they ought to be allowed to remain at school until 12 or 14 years of age at least; their present early removal has a tendency to weaken the whole system of the body and the powers of the mind.

A good national education, under the control of the Government, but not in connexion with any religious party, would be a blessing to the community.

No. 309   MR. JOHN DIXON, schoolmaster:

The school I superintend has been established about 17 or 18 years: it is in connexion with the Hirwaun Works. A halfpenny in the pound towards the school is deducted from the wages of all. The children are brought to school at about four and five years of age, and remain some until seven and others until ten years of age, as the circumstances of parents differ. Very few of the children of the colliers or firemen get beyond multiplication, but the shopkeeper's children (sic) and others who work above ground have greater advantages and continue longer at school.

It is much to be regretted that girls are taken so young to work, especially into mines; for after the work is over they exhibit no desire of instruction, are ignorant, idle, and questionable in morality, commonly being with child before marriage; and two-thirds don't know how either to sew a dress or darn their own stockings: Many are of very coarse behaviour, and swearing is common.

We have five meeting-houses in the place,[2] in most of which schools are held on the Sabbath-day; we have no church within three miles; the meeting-houses are well-attended. Of late years friendly societies have much increased; there are three lodges of Odd Fellows, one Druids, and one Ivorite, together with three female societies: these societies are of great advantage to the people in cases of sickness or accident, which are very numerous. The frequent reductions which have been made in the last three years in the wages of the working people has greatly diminished their comforts.

We had a short time since two schools, one for the miners, kept by myself, and the other for those employed in the iron-works: this latter school is not now open. The average attendance at my school is about 50; 35 males and 15 females at present attend. Many of the children are irregular in their attendance, and it is a pity that so many of the parents do not appreciate the benefits of education.

(The room in which this school is held is small and inconvenient; no ceiling, bad walls, and altogether more like a stable than a school; the place was almost surrounded with a ditch of dirty water.)

No. 310   EVAN JAMES, aged 16:

I have been employed seven years; my employment is throwing from the engine. I have never been seriously injured. I was at the Fireman's school 12 months; it has ceased now. I never could read. Goes to the Sunday-school. Has three sisters and one brother at work; none of them can read. There are 12 months in the year; cannot say how many days. Jesus Christ is the Son of God.

(Very ignorant; no knowledge of figures whatever.)

No. 311   MORGAN THOMAS, aged 15, haulier:

Have been at work eight years, and would have been at work *now* but for the loss of my left arm, which occurred four months since, when it was amputated. Mr Forest attended me. The accident occurred from the weight of the trams over-powering me, whilst I was in the act of taking a sprig out of the wheel, and the wheels passed over me. I was laid idle two months, since

In most English and Welsh sources of the 19th C. this placename is usually given the inaccurate spelling 'Hirwain'. This has been corrected throughout.

which I have been to school, and have learned to write. (Writes very well.) I did earn 9 shillings a week; I can do nothing now. During my illness and up to this time I have received 7 shillings a week from a club of which I am a member, held at Mrs Moore's, at the Cardiff Arms; but I shall soon be reduced one-half by our regulations. (A very intelligent lad.)

No. 312 GILES GILES, aged 15, engine-boy:

Was nine years old when first taken to the work; could read a little before; went to school. Am not able to do any work at present, as I lost my right arm by falling under the locomotive engine, which works between the works and the level; it occurred as I was going to pump the water; it is a little more than 12 months ago, since which time the schoolmaster has taught me to write with my left hand.

(A very intelligent lad, and great credit is due to the master for having taught him to write with his left hand better than any working lad of the same age with whom I have yet met in my present inquiry.)

No. 313 ELIZABETH WILLIAMS, aged 9:

Been below ground six months, assists to fill father's trams; does not remain underground more than six or eight hours; does not like the work at all; was first taken by father because he could get an extra tram for me; a good many girls besides me work in the mines, at pushing the trams and tipping. (Rather intelligent, and reads a little English.)

No. 314 ELIZA LEWIS, aged 16, tipper:

I have been three years at work; the labour is very hard; as when the trams are out we have to work all weathers; has never been at other work, but thinks she would prefer it, as the work would not be so fatiguing. Was at school before I went to work, and learned to read and write. (Reads English and Welsh, and writes a little, with a tolerable scriptural knowledge.)

No. 315 MARY REES, aged 15, tipper:

Does the same kind of work as Eliza Lewis; cannot say how many years she has been at work at Aberdare — pretty nearly all her life. Never was at school; sometimes goes to Sunday-school. (Very ignorant.)

No. 316 MARGARET LEWIS, aged 15, tram-oiler:

Been oiling trams 12 months; was tipping some time before; work at the mouth of the level, but not underground. I have never met with any accident, though accidents frequently occur here. Many girls are taken in the mines by their fathers before they can do much work. I earn 4s. 6d. per week. Was not able to go to school before I came to work but am now learning to read at the Wesleyan school; I can sew a little, but not much.

No. 317 MARY JACOBS, aged 14, trammer:

Works with sister, who is 16 years of age; work in the mine at pushing trams; we have both done so these three years; the work is very hard, and not very regular; sometimes we work 12 or 14, and sometimes only eight hours. We expect the men will draw us out, as the work is getting short, and then we shall have to hang about. We work on father's account. Neither I nor my sister have ever been to school, and we cannot read.

No. 318   JOHN THOMAS, aged 7, air-door boy:

Been 12 months below; don't dislike the work now; earns 6d. a day. Never was at school.

No. 319   ELIZABETH RICHARDS, aged 13, trammer:

Has wheeled coals two or three years in the mine; cannot say she knows her exact age; has never been to any school; has never been seriously injured, though often hurt so as to lay by for a day or two. Cannot read. (Very ignorant.)

No. 320   MORGAN DAVIES, aged 9, haulier:

Been two years at work; earns 8 shillings a week; has occasionally got hurt, but never laid by more than a week. Never went to any day-school; is learning a b, ab (sic).

No. 321   MARY ANN JONES, aged 18, pumper:

Pumps water below to the level; been pumping these two years; was working in the levels and tips some years before; work is very hard; work is sometimes eight, sometimes 12 hours; earns one shilling a day. (Very ignorant.)

No. 322   CHALRES FORREST, ESQ., surgeon, Hirwaun Iron-Works:

The men employed in the coal-mines are not prone to any specific or chronic organic disease which can be attributed to their avocation. Those, however, who labour in the iron-ore mines are frequently affected with chronic diseases of the chest, attributable, I believe, to the inhalation of choke-damp (carbonic acid gas), and they are more frequently the subjects of consumption than the colliers.

The men employed in the manufacture of iron are also exempt from any specific class of chronic disease, but they are very frequently the subjects of acute inflammation, particularly of the lungs, arising from the sudden and great transitions of temperature.

It is very difficult to give anything like a fair approximation to the average duration of the miners' lives in the absence of correct statistical data. I would say, however, that a collier's life is ten per cent superior to that of an iron-ore miner, because of the greater purity of the atmosphere they breathe whilst engaged at their work.

The average duration of life of those employed in the fire-works is decidedly inferior to that of the colliers and miners, say ten per cent below their standard.

Most undoubtedly the employment of very young persons underground will have a tendency *per se* to engender disease, by deteriorating the powers of the system, and so shorten the duration of life.

My observation has not led to the opinion that the rising generations are the subjects of *marked disease* consequent upon their several employments or modes of life. I would rather incline to the reverse opinion, from the extremely infrequent occurrence of scrofula amongst them — a disease which is invariably developed by any long-continued train of causes which tend to undermine the physical powers.

I am not in a condition to speak of the system pursued in this particular work, in comparison with any other, as regards the employment of young females in the mines, because I have not had the opportunity of witnessing the plans adopted in any other work.

The salubrity of this immediate locality I consider to be of a high order, the general health of the people being extremely good. Fevers and all epidemic maladies are very mild in their attacks: this was remarkably exemplified at the time the Asiatic cholera visited us,[3] the cases here being under one percent of the entire population, whilst in many parts of the principality it went as high as five or six percent.

The state of morals and the system adopted in respect of education cannot be applauded. Great improvements are called for, but which cannot be effected without a much more rigid code of discipline than is at present pursued.

I much regret it is not in my power to comply with your last inquiry, touching the number of accidents and the proportion of able-bodied men as compared with the disabled. I have never kept a record of all the accidents occurring in the works, merely making notes of remarkable cases professionally. Surgical cases of every grade, however, occur very frequently, and the loss of life and limb is fearfully and painfully felt in too many instances. The bulk of the population not having legal settlements here are of course removed to their own parishes whenever they become incapable by loss of limb or otherwise from following their work.[4] The amount, therefore, of disabled men actually living here is very trifling indeed.

I have resided here the last 17 years as surgeon to this work. The six years immediately preceding I passed in the heart of the cotton district of Lancashire, as house surgeon to a public institution, and wish to state my opinion of the decided superiority of the working masses here, as compared with those in the North of England, as regards their physical condition, and greater exemption from diseases of all kinds.

4. 'Working at the Trams': a young man bearing loaded trams on a narrow underground track as was done by Mary Jacobs, aged 14, (Franks' evidence no. 317).
Source: *Report of the Commission into the Employment of Children and Young Persons, 1842.*

FOOTNOTES:

1 The 'Independent church, Hirwaun' was Nebo chapel, established in 1821 and still functioning; see *The Religious Census of 1851: a Calendar of the Returns Relating to Wales*, by Ieuan Gwynedd Jones & David Williams (eds.), vol. 1, South Wales, U.W.P., Cardiff, 1976, p.188. For its minister and the Commission's witness see *Hanes Eglwys Annibynol Ebenezer, Aberdar*, by Jacob Treharne, Aberdar, 1898, pp.18-19, 26-27 and 96 (including a photograph); the Revd. Williams was born at Glynneath in 1807 and died at Hirwaun in 1877; in testifying to the Commission in 1841 he was a comparatively young man aged 34 years; he also appeared as a witness before the Commission of Inquiry into the State of Education in Wales (1847).

2 According to the denominational histories of the district and also the *Returns* of the religious census of 1851 there were but four 'meeting-houses in the place' which we would know as Hirwaun today: these were Nebo (Independent, established 1821); Bethel (Calvinistic Methodist, established 1823 and still in existence); Ramoth (Baptist, established 1825 and closed in December, 1986); and Soar (Wesleyan Methodist, established 1825 and closed in 1977) — see Jones & Williams (eds.), p.188. The fifth chapel to which the schoolmaster alludes may well be Ebeneser Independent church, Trecynon; this was founded in 1811 as the 'mother church' of independency in the locality, and was built as the result of a vision at Heolyfelin — a village then busily expanding onto 'comin Hirwaun' (Treharne, pp.13-15; and 'Hanes Crefydd yn Aberdar', an essay in *Llawlyfr Undeb yr Annibynwyr Cymraeg, Aberdar, 1935*, pp.37-38).

3 Asiatic cholera arrived in south Wales during 1832 and is said to have caused 160 deaths at Merthyr Tydfil (see Charles Creighton, *A History of Epidemics in Britain*, 2 vols., 1894; 2nd ed., 1965; vol. 2, p.822ff: quoted in A.C. Davies, 'The Old Poor Law in an Industrializing Parish: Aberdare 1818-1836', *Welsh History Review*, vol. 8, no. 3, (June, 1977), p.307-308). In view of Forrest's later statement that he had been resident at Hirwaun 'the last 17 years', it transpires he had arrived in or about 1824.

4 Statutory provision for dealing with the poor of a parish had existed since anti-vagrancy measures in 1388 required any parish unable to maintain an 'impotent beggar' to return him to his place of birth. From 1535 until 1930 a series of poor law acts (whether or not so entitled) made revised provision for dealing with poverty. One aspect of this was the Settlement Act of 1697. This permitted strangers to reside in a parish only as long as they possessed a settlement certificate which confirmed that their old parish (usually that of birth) would take them back if ever they came to be in need of poor relief. The non-possession of such a certificate by the labouring poor was often overlooked during the early 19th century until a labourer or his family became a charge upon the parish of their recent domicile; then, possession or otherwise of a certificate constituted grounds for the forcible removal of destitutes to their native heath. It is this practice to which Forrest refers in his testimony. The principle was not revoked by the Poor Law Amendment Act of 1834.

5. A contemporary view of the Middle Duffryn Colliery, Cwmbach, in 1852.
Notice the use of a 'whym' in the right-hand background, and the site of the
colliery alongside the Aberdare Canal along which coal was at first
transported to the Glamorganshire Canal at Abercynon and thence to
Cardiff.
Source: *Illustrated London News, 29/5/1852.*

EVIDENCE COLLECTED BY SUB-COMMISSIONER RHYS WILLIAM JONES, ESQ., IN RESPECT OF THE HIRWAUN IRON-WORKS AND THE COLLIERIES AND MINE-WORKS OF THE ABERDARE IRON COMPANY IN THE COUNTY OF GLAMORGAN:

(SOURCE: Appendix to the Report of the Royal Commission of Enquiry into the State of Children in Employment, 1842; Vol. III, Part II, pp.634-635 & 657-659):

The works at Plymouth belonging to Messrs. Hill, and Cyfarthfa belonging to Mr. Crawshay[1] have been visited by Mr. Franks. The works at Hirwaun, also belonging to Mr. Crawshay, and the small works belonging to the Gadlys Company (employing together about 1,300 persons) I consider of a character analogous to those at Aberdare and Abernant being in the same district, and I have not therefore taken any examinations of the children at them; but on my visit to Hirwaun I had the pleasure of seeing Mr. Forrest, the intelligent and talented surgeon to that works, and Mr. Dixon the schoolmaster, and I have annexed copies of the statements of both these gentlemen to the accompanying papers in the Appendix to this Report.

I have the honour to be, Gentlemen,
Your most obedient servant,
R.W. JONES

Loughor, Sept., 20th, 1841

REPORT OF C. FORREST, ESQ., SURGEON TO THE HIRWAUN IRON-WORKS. *19th MAY, 1841:*

Twenty-three years' experience and observation in the active practice of my profession (seventeen of which have been passed as surgeon to iron-works, and six as house-surgeon to a public institution in the heart of the cotton trade) have brought me to the conviction that the employment to which young persons are subjected in the mines and collieries of this district is not in any way detrimental to their physical condition; on the contrary, in a great majority of instances, the proper development of their physical powers appears to be facilitated thereby, more especially as regards young females, who are entirely occupied in out-door work; their robust frames, and the rude health they enjoy, fully justify this opinion: as contrasted with domestics and others in the rural districts, their superiority is very apparent.

The remarkable exemption from chronic diseases, more particularly scrofula, in both classes (male as well as female) is a striking proof that (as their general appearance indicates) they are both better fed and better clothed than others in the same rank of life not similarly employed with themselves. The condition of the boys who are wholly employed in the mines is in every way good; the great care and attention which is bestowed upon ventilation enable them to inhale an atmosphere quite capable to sustain all the functions of vitality in a state of due vigour and integrity: the low rate of mortality from epidemic diseases leads to this conclusion. Having from circumstances been enabled to draw a comparison between the condition of young persons employed in the manufacture of iron and that of those employed in the manufactures of the North of England, I feel it difficult to find language sufficiently forcible to express the decided superiority of those located in this district.

(Signed)   C. FORREST, Surgeon,
Hirwaun Iron-works, Merthyr Tydfil

STATEMENT OF MR. JOHN DIXON, SCHOOLMASTER AT HIRWAUN:

There are four chapels at Hirwaun, belonging to the Wesleyans, Baptists, Welsh Calvinistic Methodists, and Independents, at which places Sunday-schools are held chiefly in the Welsh language, in which reading only is taught; the diffusion of general knowledge is never resorted to.

There are two day-schools, one supported by the miners and colliers, and others dependent thereon, which school is supported by 'a poundage' of one halfpenny per pound on the miners' and colliers' monthly earnings; the other belongs to those who are called firemen, but paid in the same manner as the above — a halfpenny per pound. As I have no connexion with the firemen's school I can only notice it. The schools are situate at Hirwaun, and open from eight a.m. to five p.m. Females are not taught needlework, unless a mantua-maker may take a few private pupils. The greater part of the females are working out of doors, filling mine, cleaning and unloading the same, unloading coal at the works, and setting the coal for coking, tipping mine and rubbish, pumping in levels, etc.

In the miners and colliers' school boys are taught reading, writing and arithmetic; and there are some who have been educated in the above school who fill respectable situations, and are excellent scholars; the girls are taught reading, writing and arithmetic also.

The teacher belonging to the miners and colliers' school has had a good education, and is fully competent to teach, and certainly qualified for a higher department than where he is now situated, and gives every satisfaction to those by whom he is employed.

Children are brought to school at very early periods, say from five to six, and remain therein according to the circumstances of the parents. Generally they leave school about eight or ten years of age.

The Sunday-schools are undoubtedly beneficial to keep those children removed from the day-schools in memory of what they had learnt before, as far as reading is concerned; but as the Welsh language is what they are mostly instructed in, English readers are frequently on the decline; the Wesleyans are the only sect who adopt the English language here.

In general the children are taken from school from the ages of eight and twelve; but a great deal depends upon the parent's (sic) situation in life.

I do not consider that Sunday-schools are conducted at this place in such a mode as to make up the loss of instruction by early removal from the day-schools, partly from the reason given above, and also from the incompetency of the Sunday-school teachers, the majority of whom require instruction themselves in a great degree.[2]

The great disadvantage experienced here is the want of books adapted to expand the youthful idea; as the workmen here support the school exclusively at their own expense, they cannot afford to provide the elementary books requisite to the improvement of the mind. And there is another inconvenience in not having a school-room of their own, being obliged to pay a heavy rent for the one now in use.

The miners and colliers, as well as those belonging to the other department of the works here (Hirwaun), deserve the greatest commendation for the readiness and willingness they manifested in the formation of these schools at their own expense; I believe it is the first established upon the 'poundage' system in Wales.

It would be a very great kindness if they could by some means avail themselves of the assistance of the fund granted by Parliament for the erection of school-houses, as they would readily subscribe as much as lies in their power to further the object in view; at present they have no school-house of their own for want of funds.[3]

(Signed) JOHN DIXON
Hirwaun Works, near Merthyr Tydfil

20th May, 1841

No. 165 ABERDARE AND ABERNANT IRON-WORKS, in the parish of Aberdare, in the county of Glamorgan, belonging to the Aberdare Iron Company:[4]

STATEMENT OF CHILDREN AND YOUNG PERSONS EMPLOYED:

Total Number M F	Nature of Employment	Under 13 yrs M F	Between 13 & 18 M F	Can read	Can write	Maimed/ crippled	Remarks
13 17	At Blast Furnaces	7 3	6 14	9	1	–	2 boys 9 yrs; 1 girl 8 yrs.
76 –	At Forges & Mills	21 –	55 –	43	10	–	3 boys 10 yrs.
23 –	At the Collieries	14 –	9 –	8	3	–	2 boys 8 yrs.
151 20	At the Mine Works	47 3	104 17	102	18	–	2 boys 7 yrs.
263 37	TOTALS	89 6	174 31	162	32	–	

SUMMARY OF PERSONS EMPLOYED:

	Young Persons:		Adults:	
	M	F	M	F
At the Blast Furnaces	13	17		
At the Forges and Mills	76	—	780	80
At the Collieries	23	—		
At the Mine-works	151	20		
TOTALS:	263	37	780	80

MALES	1,043
FEMALES	117
TOTAL:	1,160[5]

Total population of the whole parish of Aberdare:		Total number of houses: 1,171; plus 46 uninhabited and 19 being built.
MALES	3,523	
FEMALES	2,938	
TOTAL:	6,461[5]	

6. A horse-driven 'whym' such as that by which John Lewis, aged 14½, told sub-commissioner R.W. Jones he had been injured in having his head 'squeezed' (R.W. Jones' evidence no. 168).
Source: "The History of the T.U.C., 1868-1968: A Pictorial Survey", London, 1968, p.29.

EXAMINATIONS TAKEN AT ABERDARE COLLIERIES AND MINE-WORKS:

No. 166 JOHN SMITH, colliery agent, aged 35 years:

I have been seven years agent; I have a great many boys in the collieries, but no girls underground. The boys go to work at eight years old; very few of them have had any school before they begin to work. I see no objection to their going to work in any way, except that they lose the opportunity of going to school. I think the only reason why they are not sent to school is because their parents cannot afford to pay for them. They mostly work for their fathers. They appear to have very good health, and seldom lose time from the works. I believe the most of them go to the Sunday-schools. Accidents very rarely occur to them. The men in the colliery and mine-works are allowed a certain numbers of trams to bring out their coal or mine, and they often can cut or dig more than those trams can bring out. When they have a boy they are allowed an extra tram, and they frequently take their boys to work only to get such extra tram.

No. 167 MARY CLEMENT, aged 13 years, and been to work three years:

I carry tools for the colliers from the top of the balance-pit to the forge and back; it is about a quarter of a mile. I go once in the morning and three times in the evening; I come out about six or seven in the morning and go back home about nine, and come again about four and stay until six or seven in the evening. I get 9d. per month from each collier; they are about 30. I get about 5s. or 6s. per week. I have never been in any school but the Sunday-schools; I go to them, and am learning to spell.

No. 168 JOHN LEWIS, aged 14½ years, and been working five years:

I am a haulier in the colliery and about the yard; I am now driving a horse in the trams, bringing red ore from the canal to the furnaces. I go out about six in the morning, and get in with the horse about five in the evening. I never work at night. I get 7s. per week. About three months back I met with an accident while I was driving a horse in a 'whym' at the colliery; I got my head squeezed, and was home for a month ill; I am not quite well yet. I can read a little, I have learned it at the Sunday-school.

No. 169 EDWARD MORGAN, aged 8 years; HENRY MORGAN, aged 13 years:

We work with our father and brother in the colliery; we fill small coals into the trams, and hand tools to our father and brother. We all of us got last month £7.9s.10d. We get 1s. per day between us. We are in the works eleven hours every day; we do not work at night. We are five children in all; two do not work. We have been in school and can spell a little in English and Welsh; we go now every Sunday. Our father cannot afford to put us in a day-school.

No. 170 DAVID THOMAS, aged 11 years, been working three years; THOMAS CLEMENT, aged nine, been working one year; ROBERT WILLIAMS, aged eight, been working one year:

We are door-boys in the colliery. David Thomas opens five doors, the other two open five doors between them; we run from one to the other before the horses, and open and shut them. We have hard work sometimes. We get 2s. 6d. per week each. We have all good health, and no accident has happened to us. We go to the Sunday-schools and are learning to read Welsh; we cannot read much yet. David Thomas's father has seven children, and Thomas Clement's four. Our fathers work in the colliery with us.

No. 171 THOMAS PHILLIPS, aged 12 years:

I am working with my brother in the mine-level; I fill the mine, he digs into the trams. We work 9 or 10 hours a day. I get enough of time to eat in the level. I do not know what I get; my father gets my money. No one ever beats the boys in the works; they sometimes fight and beat themselves, and then their fathers or brothers come upon them. I have never been beaten in the works; if I always get so good a place I shall not care. My father wants me to go to school, but I rather go to the work; it is my own fault that I do not go to school I cannot read.

No. 172 MARY JONES, aged 11 years, been 1½ years at work:

I carry tools to the men at the mine levels; I go back and forward with them to the smith; I have to go a mile; I go four or five times in the day. I have enough of time to go home to my meals. I get 3s. 6d. per week. I cannot read; I go to school on Sundays, and am beginning to learn to spell. I am quite well, and lose no time from illness.

No. 173 ELIZA EVANS, aged 19 years, been working one year:

I work in the mine level, filling the trams and helping the miner. I do nearly the same kind of work as he does; he takes the hardest work and uses the powder for blasting, but I can bore the holes, and I help to push the trams out. We work in the level about 10 hours; we sometimes come out once or twice, and sometimes not once during the turn. The miner pays me 6s. per week, and finds the light.[6] There is no particular meal-times kept in the level; we go in about six or seven o'clock in the morning, and take some bread and cheese, or butter, with us, and eat it when we like, and come out and go home to our suppers about four or five o'clock in the evening. The work agrees very well with my health, and I believe the same with all the girls. I have lost no time since I began to work. I was never in school, and cannot read. My father and mother are dead. I now lodge in the neighbourhood of the works.

No. 174 RICHARD LEWIS, aged 12 years; DAVID LEWIS, aged 16 years:

We help the miners in the levels; David has been working for seven years; he now gets 10s. per week and finds his own light. Richard gets 4s. 6d., and the miner finds light; the light costs about 6d. per week. Our father was killed in the colliery eleven years ago.[7] David has met with several accidents: he broke both his legs about two years ago, under the trams in the level, and he broke his leg once by falling off a hedge. He has been in school, and can read a little English; Richard cannot read, but they both go to the Sunday-schools, and so do most of the boys and girls.

NO. 175 WILLIAM EDMOND, aged 12 years; ISAAC RICHARD, aged 11 years:

We work in the mine-works, picking and piling mine; we work from six in the morning to six in the evening; we sometimes have meal-times, but not always. We have bread and cheese and bacon for dinner, and we drink cold tea. We work sometimes in the levels helping the miners and pushing trams. William Edmond gets 7s., and finds his light, when in the level. Isaac Richard gets 3s. 6d. and has his light found him. We have very good health, and no person abuses us. We cannot read, but we go to the Sunday-school.

No. 176 JOHN WILCOX, aged 13 years, and been working three years:

I am a haulier; I drive a horse above ground, and carrying tools; I work ten or twelve hours, and have meal-times. I was in school for three years before I came to work, and can read the Testament, but cannot write. I get 4s. 6d. per week. I have met with no accidents.

No. 177 JOHN LEWIS, aged 12 years, and been at work three years:

I work with my brother-in-law, he is a miner, and I live with him. I go regularly to the Sunday-school, and can read the Testament. My father is dead and my mother is away; my brother-in-law takes care of me.

(NOTE: The mine agent related to me a melancholy history of the family of this poor boy. His father, who was an industrious man, became asthmatic, and was for some time confined to his house at Aberdare, when one night, about three years ago, he was cruelly set upon and murdered by his own wife. She was apprehended, but made out to be insane, and is now in confinement for the crime.)

No. 178 JOHN WILLIAMS, aged 15 years, been working six years:

I am working in the mine level with my father; I assist him in getting the mine; I get about 8s. per week. We work the same time as the other miners, about ten hours a day. I have met with no accident. I have been in school a little but cannot read. I go sometimes to the Sunday-school.

No. 179 MARY BENJAMIN, aged 16 years, been at work five years:

I am now driving coal on the tram-road; I drive a team of three horses in the waggons. I am out all day, from six to six, but have meal-times. Driving horses is very hard work, as the road is steep in some places. I have not been at this work very long; I worked before at the Gadley's Mine Patch.[8] Girls do not often drive horses, but they do here sometimes. I do not like the work; I do not know what I shall get; I think about 5s. per week. I cannot read.

No. 180 JOHN REES, aged 13 years:

I am working with my father in the Gadley's Mine Patch; I assist my father; I do not know what wages I get; I have been with him for three or four years; he is a miner and works by the job. I lose a day now and then when I take cold, but not very often. My work is not very hard. We have meal-times in the patch. I have been in school, and can read a little.

FOOTNOTES

1 The Plymouth Ironworks were located at Pentrebach, Merthyr Tydfil, and originated in a lease demised by the earl of Plymouth in 1763. In 1788 the works were conveyed to Richard Hill I, brother-in-law and agent to Anthony Bacon I, the pioneer of Cyfarthfa. By 1826, Richard Hill's youngest son, Anthony, had become Managing Partner of the works and it is to him the text here refers. Anthony Hill died in 1862. The 'Mr Crawshay' mentioned was William Crawshay II, builder of Cyfarthfa Castle and later master of those ironworks. The Hirwaun works had been founded in 1757, and in 1818 were bought on behalf of the head of the Crawshay family, William I. He left their management to his son, William II, and bequeathed them along with Cyfarthfa to the latter upon his death in 1834. In 1831 William II devolved everyday management at Hirwaun to his own third son, Henry, who subsequently married a Hirwaun village-girl named Eliza Harris to the great annoyance of his father. Their first two daughters were christened by the then minister of Nebo chapel, Joseph Harrison, in 1835. Henry remained at Hirwaun until 1847 when William's second son, Francis, (already manager of their Treforest works) was put in charge and took up residence there before retiring to Sevenoaks in Kent. The novel *Y Geilwad Bach* ('The Little Wakener'), Llanelli, 1929, by Hirwaun-born Lewis Davies, is based upon the life of a young worker at the Hirwaun ironworks during Francis Crawshay's era there. Despite his great eccentricity, Francis Crawshay is said to have been very popular with the local workmen; and one factor in this may well be that he was the only member of the family ever to bother to learn Welsh.

2 While there is much in Dixon's remark from the standpoint of a professional schoolmaster, it hardly diminishes the achievement of sorely-pressed workers in organizing largely of their own resources chapels and Sunday Schools which implanted through the Bible a basic ability to read and reflect amongst the exploited of Aberdare and elsewhere. The Sunday School movement did not seek to rival or supplant day-schools. Its job was that of imparting religious enlightenment. Despite the obviously limited scope and capacity of the local Sunday Schools in instructing their attenders, it is difficult to see what more could have been achieved of their own means by the impoverished workers of 1840-42 than was already afforded by their support of both day- and Sunday tuition. Theirs was a vicious circle of ignorance by poverty and of poverty by ignorance. Education was indeed an answer; but its systematic extension was to be painfully slow. Meanwhile, the poor busied themselves as inheritors of faith. (See *Education in Industrial Wales, 1700-1900*, by L.W. Evans, Cardiff, 1971, esp. chapter IX.).

3 Prior to the Forster Act of 1870, daily education for the masses was provided (if at all) by private adventure schools and by the nonconformist British Society (founded in 1810) or the Anglican National Society (founded in 1811): both voluntary organizations. Until 1834 the state made no provision for the education of the people at large. That year, the first education grant out of public money was conceded when £24,000 was awarded between the British and National Societies. It is to this fund that Dixon here alludes. A British School was attempted at Hirwaun in 1849, but it faced severe difficulties. According to the Revd. William Roberts (Nefydd), agent of the British Society in south Wales, these arose from the obligation of the ironworkers to support from their wages two works schools; the indifference of the works manager about the education of the people (presumably meaning Francis Crawshay); the alleged lethargy of the Bute estate; and the inefficiency of the British School's own teachers, one of whom was 'a drunken man ... in the habit of cursing and swearing at the children' (L.W. Evans, op.cit., p.188).

4   The Aberdare (Llwydcoed) Ironworks originated in a lease dated February, 1800 that was to run from June, 1799, by which George and John Scale of Hansworth, Staffordshire, leased 702 acres of 'fforest Llwydcoed'. Their object was to develop an ironworks. The Abernant venture began in 1801 with leases granted to Jeremiah Homfray and James Birch of land upon which to establish their concern. In 1802 the Tappenden family of London and Kent joined the Abernant partnership; and in 1807 they entirely took over the business there. One of their advisers, Richard Fothergill I (1758-1821), witnessed the conveyance. In 1813, Abernant became bankrupt, and was purchased in 1818-1819 by the Scales of Llwydcoed. They appointed Richard Fothergill's nephew, Rowland (1794-1871), their manager at both works. In 1846 Rowland Fothergill bought out the Scales and retired soon thereafter to Hensol. The management of both Llwydcoed and Abernant then passed to Rowland's newphew, Richard Fothergill III (1822-1903), who was elected M.P. for Merthyr & Aberdare in 1868. (See John Lloyd, *The Early History of the South Wales Iron Works, 1760-1840*, London, 1906, pp.116-126; and A.C. Davies, 'The Aberdare Canal, 1793-1900', in the *Journal of Transport History*, new series IV, vol. 3, February, 1978, pp.151-153).

5   In 1841, the population of the parish of Aberdare was 6,471 — ten more than is noted here (see *Census of Great Britain, 1851: Population Tables... 1801-1851*, vol. XI, HMSO, 1852). Thus the 1,160 male and female workers stated as being in the employ of the Aberdare and Abernant ironworks represented 17.93% of the total population of the parish. The male workforce (1,043) represented about 29.6% of the overall male population (3,523). At Hirwaun and Gadlys, sub-commissioner R.W. Jones estimated that 'about 1300 persons' were in employment. Given this, it meant that 20% of the local population were employed at those works. The four local ironworks existent in 1841/42 therefore employed some 2,460 people in all, or 38% of the total population. Many of these people were coal or iron miners; and when the indeterminate number (possibly a few hundred) already working in the three or four sale-coal pits of the district are added it becomes clear how massive a presence the mining community had already established at Aberdare by 1841-42.

6   Despite the invention of the safety lamp by Sir Humphrey Davy (1778-1829) miners at Aberdare continued to use candles and open lamps well into the 1850s although the area was singled out by Herbert Mackworth, inspector of mines for south Wales, as being particularly dangerous because of its fiery seams, unsafe roofs and susceptibility to sudden emissions of gas. An explosion at Llety Siencyn, in which three men were killed and fifteen burnt, was found by Mackworth to have been caused by an unqualified overman instructing a miner to remove a pillar of coal near a seepage of gas whilst using a naked light (Mines Inspectorate *Report*, 1853, p.180; quoted in Morris and Williams, *The South Wales Coal Industry, 1840-1875*, Cardiff, 1958, p.187). The jury investigating an explosion at Thomas Powell's Middle Dyffryn colliery in 1845, when 28 people died, noted but did not condemn the use of naked lights underground (Morris & Williams, p.182). According to Mackworth, the prevalent practice among local miners was to use the safety lamp 'not... to work by, but as a test for... fire damp' (or methane); foul air being indicated by the changing appearance of the flame in the open lamp. Mackworth noted the custom throughout south Wales whereby the collier bought his own lamp as he had (and continued to buy) his own candles (Morris & Williams, p.189). Such was the practice referred to here.

7   That is, in 1830 or so. R.W. Jones' evidence was gathered in the Aberdare locality during May, 1841, and submitted to the Commissioners in September that year. The date of this fatality reminds us that while the deep mining of sale coal in the Cynon Valley begain in 1837, the labour and risks associated with digging coal are far older in the district.

8   This is the only site of mining activity referred to by name in evidence received by the Commissioners from this district. It is difficult to suggest where the 'Gadley's Mine Patch' may have been located because R.W. Jones' evidence was concerned with children employed at the Aberdare Ironworks, and specifically excluded any working for the Gadlys Iron Company. A 'patch' at this time probably indicates the digging of coal or iron-ore by surface excavation across a fairly broad stretch of hillside.

7. A contemporary view of the mouth of the Middle Duffryn Colliery, Cwmbach, where an accident occurred in May, 1852, in which 65 men and boys died.
Source: Illustrated London News, 22/5/1852.

APPENDIX

Accidents (mainly due to explosions) in the Steam Coal Collieries of the Aberdare Valley 1837-52

1843 16 August — Duffryn Colliery. Explosion of fire-damp as men were proceeding to work. Much injury done to pit but no loss of life.

1843 August-September — Ynyscynon Colliery. Two dreadfully burnt.

1844 February? — Upper Duffryn. Explosion at ventilating furnace when no one was in the mine.

1845 2 August — Old Duffryn Colliery. Explosion caused by fire-damp due to use of naked lights. 29 killed. Most died through suffocation by after-damp or through concussion (Note 4).

1845 September — Blaengwawr. Explosion of fire-damp. Several men severely burnt.

1846 July — Cwmbach. Explosion of fire-damp. Three men severely hurt.

1848 31 March — Davies' Colliery (probably Blaengwawr). Explosion. 1 killed, 2 very severely burnt

1849 May — Werfa Colliery. Explosion of fire-damp due to naked light. 3 killed, 2 not expected to survive. 12 burnt altogether. A previous explosion had occurred at the same colliery about a week before. No record of any casualties.

1849 August — Aberaman Colliery. Explosion of fire-damp caused a roof collapse. 2 severely injured.

1849 10 August — Explosion of fire-damp. 52 killed.

1850 August — Mr Wayne's Pit. Explosion of fire-damp. 2 much burnt.

1850 14 December — Middle Duffryn Colliery. Explosion of fire-damp. 13 killed.

1851 n.d. — Werfa Colliery. 14 men killed as the result of a chain breaking.

1852 May — Middle Duffryn Colliery. Explosion of fire-damp. 65 men killed.

1852 n.d. — Cwmbach Pit. Explosion of fire-damp. 2 men killed.

NOTES

1. The majority of the explosions occurred in the fiery Upper Four-foot seam.

2. In addition to the accidents listed: 'Mr Rhys (probably Mr Hopkin Rhys, a surgeon) stated that single deaths from accidents at the works were very common, being thought to average about 20 every year' (Report to Board of Health into . . . . . the Sanitary Condition of the Inhabitants of the Parish of Aberdare. T.W. Rammell. 1853. Reprinted Old Aberdare Vol. 1. P.39.

3. In an article on mining operations in Wales, dated November 10 1846, it was predicted that unless improved methods were introduced, "South Wales will undoubtedly become a huge charnel-house, before which Northumberland and Durham will sink into insignificance" Annals of Coal Mining. R.L. Galloway 1904 P.117.

4. The casualty list at the Old Duffryn Colliery included the following:

	Age
James Thomas	44
David Thomas (son)	10
John Edwards	35
William Edwards (son)	9

The above detailed have been obtained from Galloway op.cit. and through personal research.